Family ever after

igloobooks

A stormy night. Waves crash. Winds soar.
Something's washed up on the shore.

A single egg sits all alone
without a home to call its own.

One tiny mouse.
His name is Mo.
Sees the egg and cries,
"Oh-ho!"

He rolls it from the
squelchy sand...

... away from harm, upon dry land.

"It must be lost.
I'll look and see
if those birds are
its family."

"Not ours," they chirp.
"That egg is blue."

"Oh dear," says Mo.
"What shall I do?"

Mo takes it home and calls, "Hello!"
and shows his find to husband, Jo.

The egg is kept safe by the pair
who nurture it with love and care.

Until one day...

And then out pops a little beak.

A house for two,
now home for three.
Two dads. One son. A family.

Months pass by. Days filled with fun
for Mo and Jo and Boo, their son.

Birthdays shared.

And ice cream, too!

Side by side. A dream come true.

Then, one fine day, Boo stops to sigh,
"We're not the same." He wonders why.

"Look closely, Boo, and you will find families of all different kinds."

Some have two mums.

Some have one dad.

Some live with Gran,

or Uncle Brad.

Some big.

Some small.

Look, can you see?
Just two can
make a family.

Mo hugs his son. Jo strokes his head.
"Look at the things we share instead."

“The laughs. The love. The bedtime hug.
The way we all feel safe and snug.”

Family makes us who we are
and all shine brightly like a star.

Two dads. One son. A love that's shared
by different families everywhere.